THE GUIDE TO HERBS
AND SPICES

THE GUIDE TO
HERBS
AND
SPICES

CONTENTS

INTRODUCTION

Telling the difference between herbs and spices often causes confusion because they are so similar. Both are parts of plants and are used to add flavour to food. Yet most people can tell a herb from a spice and certain characteristics can be identified.

Herbs are aromatic plants. The leaves, or sometimes the whole plant, are used fresh, dried or in powder form. Parsley, chives and fennel are all herbs.

Most spices come from tropical plants, shrubs or trees. The part which is made into a spice may be the buds (cloves), the fruit (juniper berries), the bark (cinnamon), the flowers (saffron), or the roots (ginger). Spices usually need special treatment before they can be used, while herbs can be used straight from the garden. In general, spices have a stronger flavour than herbs. So there are differences between herbs and spices, yet they can be linked because both are used to flavour food.

It is always interesting to experiment with herbs and spices and it is an art to discover the perfect quantities and combinations to use in cooking. Nowadays, fresh herbs are as popular as those sold dried and many herbs can be grown successfully in the garden, on a balcony or even in the kitchen. Start with common herbs which are easy to grow. This book tells you which conditions are best for certain herbs.

ONIONS

The onion has been popular in cooking since antiquity. The Egyptians and the Babylonians were great consumers of onions, and the Greeks used it for its medicinal properties.

The onion is a bulb which is available all year round. The main types are yellow onions, red onions, spring onions, shallots and small pickling onions. The onion is protected by several layers of skin which keep it moist and preserve its pungent flavour. When an onion is peeled and chopped, moisture is released into the air and this can be irritating to the eyes.

Onions can be used in several ways in cooking. Chopped onions add flavour to salads, sauces and minced meat, and a distinctive aroma to stock. They can be browned in butter and added to many savoury dishes. Raw onions go well with many salads. Battered onion rings can be used to garnish dishes or to accompany an aperitif. Onions can also be stuffed or braised and served as a vegetable.

Spring onions are picked before the bulb forms and they have a delicate flavour. They do not keep for very long (about five days in the vegetable compartment of a refrigerator). Spring onions can also be served as vegetables or used in soups, sauces and salads.

The onion is one of the most versatile vegetables in the kitchen. It is relatively inexpensive to buy and available throughout the year.

ONION COMPOTE

9 oz (250 g) onions · butter · 1 tsp
(1 x 5 ml spoon) sugar · 2 tbsps
(2 x 15 ml spoons) red wine vinegar ·
1 glass red wine

Chop the onions finely and brown in the butter.
Sprinkle with sugar and brown for a few more
minutes. Add the vinegar and wine. Simmer for a few
minutes. This compote is delicious with meat.

ONION SALAD

1 lb 2 oz (500 g) small onions · 1¾ pints
(1 litre) salted water · juice of ½ lemon ·
4 oz (100 g) cooked ham · 2 tbsps
(2 x 15 ml spoons) sour cream · 2 tbsps
(2 x 15 ml spoons) wine vinegar ·
3 tbsps (3 x 15 ml spoons) oil · 1 tsp
(1 x 5 ml spoon) mustard · salt ·
pepper · parsley

Add the lemon juice to the salted water and bring to
the boil. Peel the onions and boil for 3 minutes. Drain
and leave to cool. Dice the ham. Mix the cream,
vinegar, oil and mustard and season with salt and
pepper. Add the onions and ham to the sauce.
Sprinkle with chopped parsley. This onion salad goes
well with cold meats.

HINTS AND TIPS

*To get rid of the smell of onions, rub your hands with
parsley or lemon juice, then wash your hands with
soap and water. If onions make you cry, peel them
under a running tap or in a bowl of water. Raw onion
stimulates the digestion and the appetite. It also helps
the large intestine to function properly and is said to
preserve youthfulness and aid the body's resistance.*

GARLIC

Garlic originated in central Asia and prefers a warm climate. It may be found growing wild in northern regions but the flavour of wild garlic is not as strong.

The stem of the garlic plant reaches a height of 40-60 centimetres. The lower part of the bulb has fibrous roots. The leaves are flat, slender and taper to a point. The tender green stem supports a flower which is white or sometimes pink. The garlic plant prefers sandy soil and a sunny position. It reaches maturity in July or August.

Garlic can be used fresh, dried or in powder form. The cloves of fresh garlic are usually crushed in a garlic crusher. They can also be crushed by sprinkling them with salt and using the flat part of a knife blade. The cloves can also be chopped into pieces or strips and used to flavour meat such as leg of lamb.

High cooking temperatures spoil the flavour of garlic, so it is best to brown it slowly in butter or oil.

Garlic butter is delicious when spread on crusty bread and heated in the oven.

Not everyone likes to use garlic because of the smell it leaves on the breath. Yet it is an excellent flavouring for soups, sauces, meat, pasta and exotic dishes. You can also rub a cut clove around the inside of a salad bowl to give a garlic flavour to salads.

GARLIC MARINADE

3 cloves garlic · salt · pepper · 5 tbsps
(5 x 15 ml spoons) oil · 3 tbsps
(3 x 15 ml spoons) wine vinegar ·
fresh parsley · ¼ bunch chives and dill ·
small handful cress

Peel the garlic and crush it in a small bowl. Add the
salt, pepper, oil, vinegar and herbs. Mix together,
cover the dish with a plate and leave to marinate for
3-4 hours in the refrigerator. This marinade adds
flavour to salads.

GARLIC MAYONNAISE

8 cloves garlic · salt · pepper · 2 egg
yolks · 9 fl oz (250 ml) olive oil · 1 tbsp
(1 x 15 ml spoon) Dijon mustard ·
2 tbsps (2 x 15 ml spoons)
lemon juice

Peel, chop and crush the garlic with a pinch of salt
and pepper. Add the mustard and egg yolks and mix
with a wooden spoon. Add a quarter of the olive oil
drop by drop, beating all the time. Then add the rest
of the oil, still beating continuously. If the mayonnaise is too thick, add a little lemon juice. This is a
delicious accompaniment to fish, salads and lamb.

HINTS AND TIPS

*Garlic has anti-bacterial action and purifies the
intestines. It is also an excellent disinfectant; one clove
of garlic chopped in a salad gives protection against
colds and flu. Garlic also purifies the blood. Whether
you like its flavour or not, garlic is good for the health.
Chlorophyll tablets taken at the end of a meal will get
rid of the smell on the breath.*

CHIVES

Chives are one of the most popular herbs. Their delicate onion flavour is delicious in many types of dish. Chopped chives are often used to garnish salads.

The chive plant grows from a bulb and its leaves reach a height of 15-30 centimetres. The leaves, or strands, are hollow, round and green. In July or August, the plant bears small, round mauve-pink flowers which can be used to garnish dishes. Chives grow well in the garden or indoors. The leaves should be cut away just above the bulbous part.

Chives should be chopped finely and added to dishes just before serving to avoid losing their delicate flavour. They are delicious in salads, soups, herb bread, sauces, egg dishes, mayonnaise and herb butter. If dried chives are plunged into hot water, they immediately regain all their flavour. Chives contain a high level of vitamin C.

Pepper soup sprinkled with chives is a culinary delight. A simple cheese flan is given extra zest by sprinkling the cheese with chives, and they are an almost indispensable ingredient of tomato salad. Chopped chives add colour to potato salad and the whole strands are used as garnish when making, for example, a bunch of red and yellow pepper strips tied together with chives.

A clump of chives will keep for several weeks indoors, provided it is watered regularly.

Chives are also ideal for freezing.

CHIVE AND RADISH SAUCE

5 fl oz (150 ml) yoghurt · 2 tbsps
(2 x 15 ml spoons) mayonnaise ·
1 bunch radishes · 1 bunch chives · salt ·
pepper · paprika

Mix the yoghurt and mayonnaise. Wash the radishes and chop finely. Wash and chop the chives. Mix together the radishes, chives, salt, pepper and a pinch of paprika. This sauce makes a delicious fondue dip and it goes well with sautéed potatoes.

TOMATO SALAD WITH SWEETCORN AND CHIVES

1 lb 2 oz (500 g) tomatoes · 1 small tin
sweetcorn · 3 tbsps (3 x 15 ml spoons)
olive oil · salt · pepper ·
½ bunch chives

Wash the tomatoes, cut into fine rings and put into a salad bowl. Drain the sweetcorn and spread the grains over the tomatoes. Mix together the olive oil, salt and pepper. Chop the chives and add to the mixture. Season well and mix lightly. A delicious accompaniment to grilled meat, fish and chicken.

HINTS AND TIPS

Like all types of onions, chives stimulate the metabolism, particularly the metabolic rate. Its leaves are a mild disinfectant. Prepare some ice with chopped chives (add the chives to the water before freezing). These ice cubes will give an unusual flavour to cool, summer drinks.

11

DILL

Dill is a member of the Umbelliferae family. A clump of dill planted near a clump of fennel (which is of the same family) will often cross-pollinate. The subtle flavour of dill is similar to that of delicate aniseed.

Dill has thin jagged leaves and bright yellow flowers. It can be sown from April to June in a sunny place. Dill seeds itself and spreads rapidly so it is a good idea to pick the seed heads before they mature. The seeds can then be left to ripen in a dry, warm and well ventilated place.

The delicate flavour of dill is lost if it is mixed with other herbs. The thin, feathery leaves are used to make sauces to serve with fish. They are also delicious in cucumber and tomato salad, or with potatoes, chicken, vegetables such as kohlrabi, haricot bean soup, sauces, yoghurt and sweet and sour dishes.

Dill seeds have more flavour than the leaves and taste a bit like cumin. They can be used to enhance lamb and pulse vegetables. They also add a certain character to cakes. A seasoning of dill and mustard is marvellous with sea salmon. Dill butter is an ideal accompaniment for grilled meat and fish. Dill also makes a good garnish.

Fresh dill will keep for a week in a closed bag in the vegetable compartment of the refrigerator. Dried dill is less aromatic than fresh dill.

HOT DILL SAUCE

2 bunches dill · 1 oz (25 g) butter ·
1 oz (25 g) flour · 16 fl oz (500 ml) meat
stock · salt · 1 egg yolk · 3 tbsps
(3 x 15 ml spoons) single cream

Wash, dry and chop the dill. Melt the butter in a saucepan and sauté half the dill without letting it brown. Stir in the flour and cook for a few minutes. Slowly stir in the stock. Continue stirring until the sauce is smooth. Reduce the heat and simmer for 5 minutes. Add salt to taste. Mix the egg yolk with the cream and add to the sauce. Cook over a gentle heat and do not allow to boil. Add the rest of the dill and serve immediately. Delicious with poached or steamed fish.

DILL BUTTER

6 oz (150 g) butter · 2 tbsps (2 x 15 ml
spoons) dill, finely chopped · salt · white
pepper · a little lemon juice

Mix the dill with the butter. Add salt, pepper and lemon juice. Stir until the mixture is smooth. If possible, shape the dill butter into a roll which can be left to harden in the refrigerator. This can then be cut into slices. Excellent with roast beef and fried fish.

HINTS AND TIPS

Dill seeds have a soothing effect. They also reduce the appetite. Fresh dill cures bad breath and an infusion of dill seeds relieves stomach pains and hiccups in children. It also helps to relieve nausea and a bloated feeling. In the past, dill was considered to be lucky and was sometimes put into wedding bouquets.

FENNEL

Fennel originated in the coastal regions of the Mediterranean basin. Its leaves can be used fresh or dried and its seeds, dried.

Fennel is also a member of the Umbelliferae family. The wild plant grows to about 1.5 metres in height. The hollow, green stem grows from a white, fleshy bulb. The outer sprigs of leaves are the most tender. These thin, feathery leaves are similar to those of dill. The umbels (umbrella-shaped heads of tiny flowers) are yellow. Fennel seeds are harvested from August to October.

The bulb, the leaves, the seeds and the umbels all smell and taste strongly of aniseed. The leaves can be used to flavour sauces, salads, meat and fish. They are also delicious on bread.

Many Italian cold meats are flavoured with fennel seeds. The seeds can also be used when preserving gherkins, pickled onions, cucumber, sauerkraut and herring. The umbels can be added to pickles.

The bulb is a complete vegetable. It can be boiled, steamed, braised or fried. The raw bulb can also be cut into thin strips and added to salads. Fennel bulb chopped finely and mixed with sausagemeat makes a tasty stuffing for chicken.

The fennel bulb goes well with many sauces, including butter sauce, hollandaise sauce or remoulade (a mixture of mayonnaise, mustard and finely chopped herbs).

MUSHROOMS WITH FENNEL SEEDS

9 oz (250 g) mushrooms · 1 tbsp
(1 x 15 ml spoon) butter · 1 tsp (1 x 5 ml
spoon) fennel seeds · salt · pepper ·
4 tsps (4 x 5 ml spoons)
sour cream

Wash the mushrooms and cut in two. Heat the butter
and fry the mushrooms quickly. Sprinkle with fennel
seeds and season with salt and pepper. Cook until the
mushrooms are tender. Add the sour cream. Simmer
for a few minutes. Delicious on toast or with pork
stew.

GRILLED MACKEREL WITH FENNEL

2 fresh mackerel, gutted · handful fennel
leaves · 2 oz (50 g) butter, melted

Rinse the mackerel in cold water. Wipe the fish dry
inside and out. Chop the fennel leaves finely and stuff
the mackerel with them. Coat the fish with melted
butter and grill for 5 minutes each side. Delicious
with French bread and a mixed salad.

HINTS AND TIPS

*Fennel is often cooked or served with fish to offset the
oily aftertaste. The essential oils in fennel stimulate the
production of gastric sugars and saliva. An infusion
of fennel is helpful for colds, stomach aches and in-
digestion. Put a teaspoon (1 x 5 ml spoon) of fennel
seeds into a cup of boiling water and leave to infuse
for a few minutes.*

CORIANDER

Coriander is native to China, India and Thailand, where it is as popular as parsley is in Europe. It is an indispensable part of Asian cookery.

Coriander is another member of the Umbelliferae family. This annual wild plant can also be cultivated, preferably in a sheltered part of the garden. It grows to a height of 70 centimetres and has a spread of 20 centimetres. The green, solid stem is straight and slender. The leaves are green and the umbels are whitish-pink. The light brown seeds are round and have a pungent aroma.

Whole or ground coriander seeds are sold in bags or jars. You can buy fresh coriander in supermarkets or in shops selling exotic foods. The Pakistanis call it 'dhania', the Moroccans 'kasbor' and the Indonesians 'ketumbar'.

Coriander appears in many oriental recipes. Ground coriander is one of the ingredients of curry powder and it is used in aromatic preservative mixtures. The flavour is slightly bitter-sweet. Coriander is often added to mixed spices.

This herb should be used sparingly otherwise its strong flavour will dominate the main food.

Coriander can be used in a number of other ways besides oriental cooking. Butter that is flavoured with chopped coriander leaves is delicious. Coriander also adds zest to cabbage, stewed apple and fruit dishes.

LAMB WITH CAULIFLOWER

2 tbsps (2 x 15 ml spoons) butter ·
1 large onion · 1 lb (450 g) lamb · 2 tsps
(2 x 5 ml spoons) ground coriander ·
2 tsps (2 x 5 ml spoons) turmeric · 1 tsp
(1 x 5 ml spoon) powdered ginger ·
2 tomatoes, chopped · 2 tsps (2 x 5 ml
spoons) yoghurt · 1 small cauliflower ·
salt · 1 tsp (1 x 15 ml spoon)
cayenne pepper

Melt the butter in a saucepan. Chop the onion finely
and brown in the butter. Dice the meat and add it to
the onion with coriander, turmeric and ginger. Mix
thoroughly and cook for 10 minutes. Then add the
chopped tomatoes and the yoghurt. Cook for a few
minutes and add cauliflower florets. Season with salt,
pepper and cayenne pepper to taste. Stir well and
moisten with a little water. Cover the pan and leave
to simmer until the cauliflower is cooked.

CURRIED COURGETTE

1 tbsp (1 x 15 ml spoon) oil · 1 tsp
(1 x 5 ml spoon) cumin seeds ·
1 courgette · ½ tsp (0.5 x 5 ml spoon)
cayenne pepper · 1 tsp (1 x 5 ml spoon)
ground coriander · 4 tomatoes · salt ·
1 sprig coriander

Heat the oil in a frying pan and sauté the cumin
seeds. Slice the courgette thinly and add to the pan.
Season with cayenne pepper and coriander. Mix
thoroughly, then add the chopped tomatoes and salt
to taste. Cover the pan and simmer for 10 minutes.
Sprinkle with chopped coriander leaves before serving.

HINTS AND TIPS

*Coriander will keep fresh for four days in a plastic bag
in the vegetable compartment of the refrigerator.*

TARRAGON

Tarragon probably originated in Siberia and Mongolia. Its name first appears in texts dating from the Middle Ages. Tarragon was brought to France from eastern Europe in the 17th century. There are two varieties of tarragon, Russian tarragon and French tarragon.

French tarragon has a very distinctive flavour. It is most often grown for making vinegars and sauce tartare. The aroma of Russian tarragon is more subtle.

Tarragon is sometimes called the dragon herb, probably because its roots look like snakes. It was supposed to be an effective remedy for poisonous bites, particularly snake bites. It is a hardy plant which can grow to 100 centimetres in height and spread 50 centimetres. Tarragon has thin, dark green leaves and a slender stem.

The distinctive flavour of tarragon is brought out by acids, particularly lemon juice or vinegar. Finely chopped fresh tarragon leaves add flavour to mayonnaise, seasoning, herb butter, sauces and marinades. Chopped tarragon enhances grilled meat, cheese and egg dishes, and tomatoes, and is an excellent addition when pickling gherkins and onions.

This herb is a versatile cooking ingredient. Tarragon chicken (an Italian recipe), tarragon butter, tarragon seasoning and brown tarragon sauces are all classics of the culinary art. Ice cream made with yoghurt and orange, and flavoured with fresh tarragon is delicious. Tarragon should be used sparingly because of its strong flavour.

TARRAGON BUTTER

4 oz (100 g) butter · 2 tbsps (2 x 15 ml
spoons) fresh tarragon, chopped · 1 tsp
(1 x 5 ml spoon) lemon juice ·
pepper · salt

Beat the butter throughly until it is soft. Stir in the
lemon juice drop by drop and add the tarragon.
Season with salt and pepper to taste.

TARRAGON VINEGAR

1¾ pints (1 litre) wine vinegar · 1 lemon ·
3 cloves · 2 tbsps (2 x 15 ml spoons)
fresh tarragon · 3 sprigs tarragon

Rinse and dry the tarragon. Remove the leaves from
the 3 sprigs of tarragon. Wash the lemon and grate
the zest (only the yellow peel). Put the tarragon
leaves and all the other ingredients into a clean bottle
and add the wine vinegar. Seal the bottle and leave it
on a windowsill in an even temperature for 2 weeks.
After this time, filter the vinegar and decant it into a
clean bottle.

TARRAGON SEASONING

4 tbsps (4 x 15 ml spoons) olive oil ·
2 tbsps (2 x 15 ml spoons) tarragon
vinegar · 1 tsp (1 x 5 ml spoon) fresh
tarragon, finely chopped · salt · pepper

Mix all the ingredients and leave them to stand for at
least 2 hours.

HINTS AND TIPS

*Fresh tarragon keeps very well in vinegar. Before
using, rinse thoroughly in cold water.*

BAY LEAVES

The bay tree, also called the bay laurel, is a native of Asia Minor and southern Europe. In northern regions, it is cultivated in greenhouses. In ancient times, the laurel wreath was placed on the heads of those deserving praise. The Roman word for to praise is 'laudare'.

The bay tree is a shrub or small tree which reaches a height of 5 metres and a span of 2 metres. The trunk and branches are woody. The dark green leaves are tough and slender. The bay tree should be planted in spring in a sunny, sheltered place. It should be protected from frost in winter. The tree grows very slowly. In fact, it makes a very attractive indoor plant.

Young bay leaves, fresh or dried, can be used to flavour soups, marinades, meat dishes, fish or vegetables (especially cabbage and beetroot), sauces, preserves and pickles. They blend very well with other herbs such as parsley and thyme.

Dried bay leaves should be stored away from the light in a sealed container. They will then keep their flavour for two years or more. Crushed bay leaves do not keep for so long. Leaves picked fresh from a tree cultivated in the garden have the strongest flavour.

Bay leaves should be used sparingly because their strong flavour will dominate the main food. The very young leaves are best used fresh. They have a spicy, bitter flavour.

LIVER AND BAY
LEAF KEBABS

8 oz (225 g) pig's liver, diced ·
handful fresh young bay leaves ·
salt · olive oil

Rinse the bay leaves under the cold tap and pat dry
with kitchen paper. Alternate bay leaves and diced
liver on skewers. Sprinkle with salt and pepper, and
coat the kebabs with olive oil. Cook under the grill or
on a barbecue.

MARINATED HERRINGS

4 smoked herrings · 2 onions · 1 sweet
and sour gherkin · a few sprigs dill ·
1 tsp (1 x 5 ml spoon) capers · 2 bay
leaves · 2 cloves · 10 black peppercorns ·
¼ pint (5 fl oz) wine vinegar · salt ·
pepper · 1 tsp (1 x 5 ml spoon) sugar

Rinse the herrings in cold water and dry them with
kitchen paper. Slice the onions and the gherkin, and
chop the dill. Put these into a clean glass jar with the
capers and the herrings. Put the wine vinegar, the bay
leaves, cloves, peppercorns and sugar into a saucepan and bring to the boil. Boil for a few minutes then
remove from the heat and leave to cool. Pour the
mixture into the jar and seal with cellophane. Leave
in a cool place for 24 hours. Drain the herrings before
serving. Delicious with rye bread.

HINTS AND TIPS

*The flavour of rice is retained if you put a bay leaf
into the rice packet. Bay leaves are effective against
bruises and contusions.*

MARJORAM

There are several types of marjoram. Sweet marjoram is a cultivated variety of wild oregano. It is an annual plant which originated in central Europe. Wild marjoram, or oregano, is a hardy plant which is native to the Mediterranean basin.

The marjoram plant grows to a height of 20 centimetres and spreads 15 centimetres. The stem, which is woody at the base, branches out as it grows. The base of the stem is brown, becoming green higher up. The tender leaves are grey-green and oval. Marjoram has a mass of small whitish-pink flowers, and small, round dark brown seeds.

Marjoram can be used on its own or mixed with other herbs. It goes well with soups, sauces, mince, peas, potatoes, meat and casseroles, eggs and cheese. Sweet marjoram makes an ideal seasoning for sausage-meat and stuffings.

Oregano is excellent in pizzas and pasta. It has a very strong flavour so it should be used sparingly.

A teaspoon of marjoram added to the cooking water gives potatoes a distinctive flavour. Marjoram can also be used to flavour vinegar. A teaspoon of dried oregano or marjoram transforms a fruit salad. Leave it to infuse for a few minutes before serving.

Dried marjoram and oregano will keep for about 3 months in a sealed jar.

MARJORAM POTATOES

2¼ lb (1 kg) potatoes · 1 onion · salt ·
pepper · 2 tsps (2 x 5 ml spoons) fresh
marjoram, chopped · 8 fl oz (250 ml)
meat stock · a few sprigs parsley

Wash, peel and dice the potatoes. Chop the onion
and fry in a little oil until golden. Add the diced
potatoes. Season with salt and pepper. Heat the stock
and pour onto the potatoes. Cover the pan and
simmer for 15 minutes. Then pour the potato mixture
into an ovenware dish. Dot with butter and brown
under a preheated grill. Delicious with roast pork and
a green salad.

SAUCE PROVENCALE

2 onions · 1 clove garlic · 9 oz (250 g)
tomatoes · 2 tsps (2 x 5 ml spoons)
marjoram · 3 tbsps (3 x 15 ml spoons)
olive oil · 1 glass white wine · pepper ·
salt · parsley · 8 fl oz (250 ml) stock

Peel and chop the onions. Crush the garlic. Peel the
tomatoes, remove the juice and seeds, and cut the
flesh into pieces. Heat the olive oil and fry the onions
and garlic until golden. Add the tomato pieces and
marjoram. Brown for a few minutes, stirring constantly.
Heat the stock, season with salt and pepper and add
to the pan. Cook, uncovered, over a high flame until
the mixture reduces to the consistency of a sauce.
Add the wine at the end of the cooking time.

HINTS AND TIPS

*Marjoram tea is an effective treatment for stomach
ache. Put 1 teaspoon (1 x 5 ml spoon) of dried marjoram into a cup and add boiling water. Leave to
infuse for a few minutes and drink in small sips.*

PARSLEY

Parsley is a well-known herb which is a member of the Umbelliferae family. It has been used since ancient times and probably originated in the Mediterranean basin.

Parsley is a biennial plant which grows to a height of 30 centimetres and spreads 20 centimetres. The root is white and the tender stem is green. The leaves are green and curly and the flowers yellow or greenish-yellow. Parsley grows best in damp, well fertilised soil in a sheltered place. It can also be grown indoors. It is rich in vitamin A and iron.

The leaves are used most often but the stems and roots can also be used in cooking. Parsley is an excellent plant for flavouring and garnishing a variety of dishes. However, parsley loses its flavour when cooked so it is best to add it towards the end or just before serving. Parsley is used to flavour soups, sauces, stews, fish dishes, chicken, eggs, salads, vegetables and potatoes. Flat-leaved parsley has a slightly less pronounced flavour than curled parsley. Curled parsley is best for garnish. Parsley sprigs can be fried or left raw for garnishing.

Parsley can also be cooked as a vegetable. Brown a shallot and a few large bunches of parsley in melted butter. Cook gently to let the parsley reduce and serve like spinach.

Dried parsley keeps for about 3 months. After this, it begins to lose its aroma and flavour.

PARSLEY SAUCE

4 oz (100 g) butter · 1 oz (25 g) flour ·
16 fl oz (500 ml) chicken stock · 1 bunch
parsley · a little lemon juice · 1 tbsp (1 x
15 ml spoon) white wine · salt · 3 fl oz
(100 ml) single cream

Melt 1 oz (25 g) butter in a frying pan. Add the flour
and cook until it has been completely absorbed.
Slowly add the stock and wine, stirring continuously.
Continue to mix until the sauce is smooth. Add the
rest of the butter to the sauce and season with salt.
Chop the parsley finely and add it to the sauce with
the lemon juice and the cream. Serve very hot as an
accompaniment to dishes such as fish and boiled or
grilled meat.

PARSLEY POTATOES

hot boiled potatoes · 2 oz (50 g) butter ·
a few sprigs of fresh parsley

Place the hot potatoes in a dish. Heat the butter and
pour it on to the potatoes. Chop the parsley finely
and sprinkle on to the buttered potatoes. Potatoes
prepared in this way are delicious when served with
fish or meat.
Use firm or, preferably, new potatoes, and if you
wash them thoroughly instead of removing the skin,
you will retain much of their nutritive value. Avoid
floury potatoes and do not over boil.

HINTS AND TIPS

*Parsley stimulates the appetite and is a diuretic and
purifier. It also stimulates digestion. The leaves keep
best if they are separated from the stems, dried and put
into a sealed container in the refrigerator. Chewing
parsley freshens the breath.*

HORSERADISH

A native plant of eastern Europe, horseradish is now found all over Europe, either cultivated or in its wild state. It is an aromatic condiment with a very strong flavour. When it is peeled and grated, horseradish exudes essential oils which can be very irritating to the mucus in the nose and the eyes.

Horseradish is a hardy plant of the Cruciferae family. It grows to a height of about 70 centimetres and has a spread of 100 centimetres. It has attractive wavy leaves and a fleshy white root which anchors itself firmly in the soil. Horseradish is an extremely hardy plant and it is very difficult to get rid of. The smallest piece of broken off root, remaining in the ground, will grow into a new plant.

The root is the only part of the plant which is used. It is usually grated to bring out the spicy flavour. Grated horseradish is available in pots.

Horseradish can be added to soups and sauces, and meat, chicken, vegetables, egg and fish dishes. It can also be used as a flavouring when preserving beetroot and pickles.

Horseradish loses its flavour during cooking so it should be added right at the end, just before serving.

Horseradish is also available in powder form. Add a little lemon juice or vinegar to freshly chopped horse-radish to stop it turning brown. A cut root will keep very well in a little damp sand or in water.

HOT HORSERADISH SAUCE

1 oz (25 g) butter · 1 oz (25 g) flour ·
1 onion · 27 fl oz (750 ml) meat stock ·
2 tbsps (2 x 15 ml spoons) grated
horseradish · salt · juice of ½ lemon ·
5 fl oz (150 ml) single cream

Chop the onion. Melt the butter in a saucepan. Add
the onion and then the flour and cook until golden.
Heat the stock in another pan and slowly add it to the
onion mixture. Stir until the sauce is smooth and
creamy. Add the horseradish, a pinch of salt and the
lemon juice, then add the cream, stirring continuously.
Reheat the sauce and serve immediately. This goes
well with boiled beef, oxtail or chops.

HORSERADISH BUTTER

4 oz (100 g) butter · 3 sprigs parsley ·
2 tbsps (2 x 15 ml spoons) grated
horseradish · salt · pepper · a little sugar ·
1 tsp (1 x 5 ml spoon) lemon juice

Put the butter in a small dish and leave it to soften in
a warm place. Wash and dry the parsley and chop it
finely. Mix the chopped parsley and horseradish into
the softened butter. Add the salt, pepper, sugar and
lemon juice and mix well. Leave the butter to harden
in the refrigerator or shape it into a roll. Cut the
butter mixture into slices. It is delicious with fish,
chicken and grilled meat.

HINTS AND TIPS

*Grated horseradish stimulates the digestion. Studies
have shown that the pungent substance contained in
horseradish is a strong antiseptic agent. Horseradish is
sometimes called the penicillin of the garden.*

THYME

Thyme was brought to northern Europe by the Romans. It is found all over the coastal areas of the Mediterranean basin and has become acclimatised to the whole of Europe. It thrives in the south of France where it has always grown wild.

Thyme belongs to the Labiatae family. The plant grows to a height of 20-40 centimetres and spreads 20-40 centimetres. Its woody stems are covered with groups of small grey-green oval leaves. If you plan to grow thyme in your garden, you can choose between hardy thyme (which is a dwarf tree) and the annual plant. The annual thyme plant has more scent.

The leaves can be used fresh or dried. Dried thyme is also available in powder form. Thyme makes an excellent flavouring for stock, soups, particularly potato, pea and lentil soups, meat, fish, chicken, vegetables, Italian sauces and rabbit. It also adds savour to tomatoes, cheese dishes, marinades, vinegar and salad dressings. Throw a handful of thyme on the barbecue to flavour the meat.

Thyme is an important part of a bouquet garni. The classic bouquet garni is made up in the following way: 1 sprig thyme; 1 bay leaf; 1 carrot; a few sprigs parsley. The bouquet is tied in a thin cotton bag and infuses as the dish cooks. It is removed after cooking. Since thyme has a strong flavour, it should be used sparingly.

TOMATOES STUFFED WITH EGG

4 tomatoes · salt · pepper · dried thyme ·
butter · 4 eggs · a pinch parsley

Wash and dry the tomatoes, cut off the tops and scoop them out with a teaspoon. Turn them upside-down to drain. Sprinkle the insides with salt, pepper and thyme. Put a knob of butter in each tomato. Grease 4 ramekins with butter. Put a tomato into each ramekin and crack an egg into it. Place the ramekins in the centre of a preheated oven (220°C/425°F/Gas Mark 7) for 10 minutes.

BRAISED RABBIT

1 rabbit (3½ lb/1500 g), dressed and cut
into pieces · salt · pepper · 4 tbsps (4 x
15 ml spoons) mustard · zest of 1 lemon ·
6 slices fatty bacon · 2 oz (50 g) butter ·
2 sprigs thyme · 4½ fl oz (125 ml) meat
stock · 1 glass white wine · salt · pepper

Coat the rabbit pieces with salt and mustard, and sprinkle with grated lemon zest. Cover the rabbit pieces with the bacon. Melt the butter in a saucepan and brown the rabbit. Add the thyme, stock and wine. Bring to the boil and season with salt and pepper to taste. Leave to simmer for 1½ hours. Put the meat in a dish, strain the liquid and pour over the meat. Delicious with potatoes, peas and stewed apple.

HINTS AND TIPS

Thyme tea is effective against colds (½ teaspoon/0.5 x 5 ml spoon of thyme per cup). A concentrated infusion of thyme tea helps to relieve a cold, or it can be added to bath water.

BASIL

Basil, which used to be called 'the herb of kings', is a native of India, though it has adapted to the climate of the Mediterranean basin. It has a very distinctive flavour which not everyone likes.

Basil is an annual of the Labiatae family. It can be grown in the garden or in pots on a balcony or indoors. It grows to a height of 90 centimetres and has a spread of 50 centimetres. Basil has a tough green stem and slender green leaves which grow to about 5 centimetres in length. They should be picked before the plant flowers.

Basil, which can be used fresh or dried, goes very well with soups, salads, sauces, fish, pulses, vegetables, crudités and meat. It is used in many Italian dishes and is one of the main ingredients of Italian pesto sauce. It blends very well with garlic and thyme.

Like many other herbs, basil has a strong flavour which can dominate a dish and so it should be used sparingly. Vinegar and oil subtly flavoured with basil can be used in many dishes.

Dried basil kept in a sealed pot will retain its scent and flavour for 6 months. Basil can also be frozen, but it does not last so well in the refrigerator. A bunch of fresh basil keeps best in oil.

PESTO

4 oz (100 g) fresh basil leaves · 2 cloves
garlic, crushed · salt · 4 oz (100 g) grated
Parmesan · 2 oz (50 g) pine kernels ·
6 tbsps (6 x 15 ml spoons) olive oil ·
pepper

Pesto is used to flavour soups, pasta and meat.
The basil must be extremely fresh. Wash, dry and
chop the basil very finely. Put it into a mortar and
add the garlic. Pound together with a pestle. Add salt,
Parmesan cheese, pine kernels, olive oil and pepper.
Crush and mix thoroughly. Put the pesto into a container, seal tightly and keep in the refrigerator.

TOMATO SAUCE WITH BASIL

1 lb 4 oz (550 g) tomatoes · 1 onion ·
1 clove garlic · a knob of butter · juice of
½ lemon · 1 tsp (1 x 5 ml spoon) chicken
stock-cube · 6 basil leaves or ½ tsp (0.5 x
5 ml spoon) dried basil · salt · pepper ·
paprika

Peel the tomatoes, remove the seeds and coarsely
chop the flesh. Peel and chop the onion and garlic.
Melt a little butter in a saucepan and add the tomatoes,
onion and garlic. Add the lemon juice and stock-
cube. Check the flavour. Simmer for 10 minutes.
Strain the sauce, then add the chopped basil, salt,
pepper and paprika.

HINTS AND TIPS

*An infusion of dried basil relieves nausea and stomach
aches (1 tsp/1 x 5 ml spoon dried basil per cup of boiling water). Fresh basil leaves have a relaxing effect.*

SAVORY

Although it is a native of southern Europe, nowadays savory is cultivated in more northern regions. It appears amongst the aromatic plants used in antiquity. The Romans, for example, drank infusions of savory for its reputed aphrodisiac properties. It has a peppery flavour and so it is also known as 'the pepper herb'.

Savory is an annual of the Labiatae family. There are two varieties, winter savory and summer savory. The plants, which are similar in appearance, grow to about 30 centimetres in height and have a spread of 15 centimetres. The stem is dark green and straight. The flowers are pink or lilac and the slender grey-green leaves are oily. Savory grows into a small shrub. Both varieties grow best in open, sunny conditions.

Savory leaves are used fresh or dried. The herb goes well with vegetables such as broad beans, haricot beans and mange-tout. It imparts flavour to ratatouille, meat and game, tomato and cucumber salad, fish and stuffing for chicken. It can also be used when pickling gherkins and to flavour oil and vinegar. Like all strong-tasting herbs, savory should be used sparingly. Its spicy, peppery flavour (which is reminiscent of thyme) is not altered by cooking.
Dried savory will keep for one and a half years in a dry place out of direct light.

BEAN SOUP

1 lb 2 oz (500 g) green beans ·
6 oz (150 g) potatoes · 1¾ pints (1 litre)
meat stock · a little flour · 2 tbsps
(2 x 15 ml spoons) dried savory ·
1 small glass sour cream ·
salt

Top and tail the beans, slice and cut into pieces. Peel
the potatoes and cut them into pieces. Cook the
beans, potatoes and savory in the stock. Blend the
soup in a liquidiser and thicken with the flour mixed
with a little cold stock. Simmer for 10 minutes. Season
with salt and add the sour cream before serving. Cut
up a few Frankfurters and add the pieces to the soup
for an interesting combination of flavours.

BRAISED PEAS

1 onion · 2 oz (50 g) butter · 1 lb 2 oz
(500 g) peas, freshly shelled · 1 sprig
savory · a little sugar · salt ·
pepper

Peel and chop the onion. Melt the butter in a saucepan and brown the onion. Add the peas, savory,
sugar, salt and pepper. Moisten with a little water
and cook gently for 10 minutes. Remove the sprig of
savory before serving.

HINTS AND TIPS

*Savory stimulates the appetite and the digestion. Its
peppery flavour makes it a useful seasoning herb
which can be used as an alternative to pepper.*

MINT

Mint is native to southern Europe but it now grows all over Europe. There are several cultivated and wild species but the best known is garden mint.

Garden mint is a hardy plant of the Labiatae family which grows to 50 centimetres. It spreads rapidly in gardens and is best contained in a pot. The green stem is square with a sturdy base. The leaves are bright green. In autumn, the plant produces small purple flowers.

Mint leaves can be used fresh or dried, and sometimes combined with other herbs, to flavour sauces, soups, roasts, salads, chutney, long drinks, jellies, tea and ice cream. It gives a delicious flavour to new potatoes and can also be added to crème fraîche or yoghurt.
Mint cream is delicious with strawberry fruit salad. Chopped mint leaves are mixed with whipped cream.
You can also buy mint oil which is extracted from the leaves and stems. It should be heated slowly and left to infuse in the same way as mint tea. Allow to cool before serving.
Mint julep is a well-known drink made with whisky, fresh mint and ice. In the past, the classic mint julep was served in a silver goblet.
Mint has a very characteristic flavour. Mint sauce is a popular accompaniment to lamb. Mint leaves are also used as garnish.

MINT SAUCE

2 oz (50 g) fresh mint leaves · 4 fl oz
(100 ml) boiling water · 1 oz (25 g)
castor sugar · 4½ fl oz (125 ml) wine
vinegar · salt

Chop the mint leaves finely and pour the boiling
water over them. Add the sugar and leave the mixture
to cool. Add the vinegar and a pinch of salt. Serve
with roast lamb.

MINT JULEP

10 ice cubes · 3 sprigs fresh mint ·
2½ fl oz (60 ml) Bourbon whisky

Crush the ice and pour into a large glass. Remove the
mint leaves from the stalks and put them into the
glass. Add the whisky and stir gently. Decorate the
glass with a sprig of mint.

MINT TEA

Mint tea is a particularly refreshing drink. Use 1 teaspoon (1 x 5 ml spoon) of dried mint or 10 fresh mint
leaves for one cup of boiling water. In Morocco, mint
tea is made by mixing a large handful of mint leaves
with China tea.

HINTS AND TIPS

*The aromatic properties of mint stimulate the brain.
Yet the refreshing flavour of mint also has a calming
effect.
Stains on the skin can be removed by rubbing with
fresh mint leaves.*

SAGE

Sage originally came from southern Europe, Spain and western Yugoslavia. Wild sage grows prolifically in the Mediterranean basin but the plant has also become acclimatised to other regions.

Sage is a member of the Labiatae family. It is very easy to grow in a sunny part of the garden. In winter, it should be protected against frost and ice. It grows to a height of 75 centimetres and its spread is about the same. It has been cultivated for such a long time that there are now many different varieties. There are differences in the colour of the leaves, the colour of the flowers, the flavour, the scent and the size of the plants.

Sage leaves can be used fresh or dried. Dried sage has a stronger flavour than fresh sage. It can be used with chicken, game, pork and liver, and in stuffing (particularly for turkey or goose). Sage also imparts flavour to marinades, salads, sausagemeat, pasta, cheese, wine vinegar and tea. Sage makes a good foil for rich, fatty meats such as goose, duck, eel and pork. When combined with other herbs, it adds savour to mutton and lamb. Its flavour is rather like mint with a hint of camphor.

One of the oldest recipes using sage is Saltimbocca alla Romana. As its name indicates, it is a Roman recipe. It consists of escalopes of veal stuffed with ham and sage. Saltimbocca is delicious served with spinach or cauliflower and potatoes or pasta.

SALTIMBOCCA

4 thin escalopes of veal · juice of
1 lemon · salt · pepper · 4 slices of raw
ham · 12 fresh sage leaves · 2 oz (50 g)
butter · 2½ pints (1½ litres) dry
white wine

Flatten the escalopes and season with lemon juice, salt and pepper. Put a slice of ham and 3 sage leaves on each escalope. Fold the escalopes in half and secure with a cocktail stick. Heat the butter in a frying pan and brown the escalopes on both sides. Add the wine and simmer for 15 minutes.

EEL SOUP

1 lb 2 oz (500 g) fresh eel · juice of
1 lemon · carrots · leeks · celery · 2 onions ·
1 oz (25 g) butter · 2 tomatoes · 1¾ pints
(1 litre) water · salt · pepper · 2 egg yolks ·
1 small pot single cream · 1 tsp (1 x 5 ml
spoon) chopped sage leaves

Clean the eel and cut into pieces 3 cm long. Season with lemon juice and salt. Chop the vegetables and onions finely. Heat the butter and brown the vegetables and onion. Peel and coarsely chop the tomatoes. Add the eel pieces and the tomatoes to the vegetable mixture and cook for 5 minutes. Meanwhile, bring the water to the boil. Add it to the mixture and season with salt and pepper. Simmer until the eel is tender. Beat the egg yolks with the cream and add the liquid to the soup.

HINTS AND TIPS

Gargling with sage tea helps to relieve mouth and throat infections.

CINNAMON

The spice is the dried bark from the twigs of the cinnamon tree. There are two sorts of cinnamon, Ceylon cinammon and Chinese cinnamon. This spice was one of the condiments used in ancient times. Chinese texts dating back to 2500 BC mention its culinary uses.

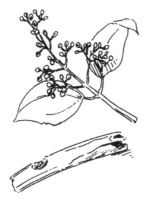

Ceylon cinnamon is a delicious spice. It is light brown and comes in the form of small sticks of bark. Chinese cinnamon is usually ground and mixed with Ceylon cinnamon.

In the oriental kitchen, cinnamon is often associated with meat. Cinnamon sticks can be infused to give flavour to sweet dishes and hot drinks such as punch, mulled wine and hot chocolate.

Ground cinnamon adds flavour to pastries and sweet rice dishes. Ceylon cinnamon is often used in the manufacture of liqueurs, such as Crème de Cacao, Angostura Bitters and Chartreuse.

Ground cinnamon can be mixed with sugar and sprinkled on desserts such as apple fritters. It is also used to add savour to rice, fish, chicken and ham.

Essential oil is extracted from cinnamon bark. This essence is used in some perfumes and in the pharmaceutical industry.

ZABAGLIONE

In Italy, the birth of a baby used to be celebrated with
zabaglione. Zabaglione sometimes appears on restau-
rant menus as a dessert but home-made zabaglione is
more like the original Italian drink which would have
been handed round after a birth.

1 tsp (1 x 5 ml spoon) cinnamon ·
10 cloves · zest of 1 lemon, grated ·
7 fl oz (200 ml) water · 7 egg yolks ·
4 oz (100g) sugar · 1 tbsp (1 x 15 ml
spoon) eau-de-vie · 1 bottle white wine

Put the cinnamon, cloves and lemon zest into the
water. Infuse for 1 hour. Filter the water. Beat the egg
yolks and sugar until the mixture becomes frothy. Still
beating, add the spice-flavoured water. Add the eau-
de-vie. Put the container into a saucepan of boiling
water. Still beating, add the wine. Continue to beat to
thicken the zabaglione

APPLES WITH CINNAMON

1 lb 2 oz (500 g) pippin apples · 2 oz
(50 g) butter · 4 tbsps (4 x 15 ml spoons)
white wine · 4 oz (100 g) sugar · 2 tsps
(2 x 5 ml spoons) ground cinnamon

Peel and core the apples, then cut into quarters. Melt
the butter in a saucepan, add the apple and moisten
with the white wine. Cover the pan and cook for 10
minutes, stirring from time to time. Mix the sugar and
cinnamon together and sprinkle the apples with this
mixture. Arrange in a dish and serve hot.

HINTS AND TIPS

*A mixture of dry rice and cinnamon cures diarrhoea.
Cinnamon stimulates the digestive system.*

GINGER

Ginger is the root of an oriental reed. According to legend, Marco Polo discovered these hollow roots when he visited China at the end of the 13th century. The plant is cultivated in Asia, western India, Indonesia, West Africa and Brazil.

Root ginger can be used fresh, dried, ground or crystallised. You can also buy ginger in syrup and ginger syrup. The most delicately flavoured ginger comes from young roots.

In Chinese and Indonesian cooking, fresh ginger is often combined with other spices. Root ginger can be grated or cut into pieces. The pieces are removed after cooking.

Nowadays, root ginger can be bought in most grocers and in supermarkets. The flavour is somewhat sharp, but the aroma is more subtle.

Ginger can be used to flavour meat, pastries, preserves, puddings, flans, fondant, vegetables, soups and sauces. It can also be added to oil and herb vinegar.

Ginger is used in the manufacture of some liqueurs and, of course, in ginger beer and ginger ale.

Root ginger has therapeutic qualities. It stimulates the appetite and the digestion as well as improving the functioning of the nerves and the gastric glands.

GINGER COCKTAIL

1 small piece ginger · 3 ice cubes · juice
of 1 lemon · 1 tsp (1 x 5 ml spoon)
golden syrup · ginger ale

Chop the ginger finely. Put it into a cocktail shaker
with the other ingredients. Shake vigorously and pour
the cocktail into a tall glass. Top up with ginger ale.

PEACHES WITH GINGER

8 tinned peach halves · 6 tbsps (6 x
15 ml spoons) ginger syrup · juice of
½ orange · juice of ½ lemon · pinch
cinnamon · 1 oz (25 g) chopped
almonds · cream to garnish

Drain the peaches and arrange in four individual
bowls. Mix the ginger syrup, lemon juice, orange
juice and cinnamon. Pour the mixture on to the
peaches. Sprinkle with chopped almonds and top
with a little cream.

NUTMEG

Nutmeg is the seed of a tropical tree which often lives to be 100 years old and grows to a height of 18 metres.

The tree has dark yellow fruit containing a seed protected by a red fleshy covering, the aril. The dried aril is mace, which is another spice. If the nutmeg seeds are white, this simply means that they have been picked early to prevent them germinating and to protect them from insects.

You can buy whole or powdered nutmeg, but it is best to buy it whole and grate it yourself. There are various types of nutmeg graters to choose from.

Grated nutmeg is used to flavour vegetables such as cauliflower, endive, kohlrabi and haricot beans. It also adds savour to sauces, potato dishes, meat, fish and cakes. Nutmeg can be included in sausagemeat or sprinkled onto pasta dishes such as Spaghetti alla Carbonara.

Nutmeg has a slightly soporific effect which is why it is used to flavour grog.

It is toxic if taken in large quantities and brings on sweating and irritability. If used in normal, small doses, however, it has a beneficial effect on the stomach.

APPLE FRITTERS

4 pippins · 6 oz (150 g) flour · 8 fl oz
(250 ml) beer · 1 egg, separated · 3 oz
(85 g) castor sugar · salt · nutmeg · 1 tsp
(1 x 5 ml spoon) oil · oil for frying ·
sugar mixed with cinnamon

Peel and core the apples and cut them into slices. Mix
together the flour, beer, egg yolk, sugar, a pinch of
salt and of nutmeg, with the oil. Beat the egg white
until stiff and fold it delicately into the mixture. Dip
the apple slices in the mixture and fry the fritters a few
at a time. Leave to drain on kitchen paper. Sprinkle
the fritters with the sugar and cinnamon mixture.

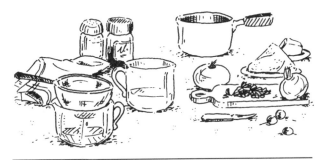

BECHAMEL SAUCE

2 oz (50 g) butter · 2 oz (50 g) flour ·
8 fl oz (250 ml) milk · 8 fl oz (250 ml)
stock · salt · pepper · 1 small onion ·
grated nutmeg · pinch thyme

Chop the onion. Heat the milk, and let the onion,
pepper, salt, nutmeg and thyme infuse in it for 20
minutes. Strain the milk. Melt the butter in a
saucepan. Add the flour, stirring all the time until
the butter and flour have combined. Gradually pour
in the stock and the milk, stirring continuously, until
the sauce is smooth and creamy. Season with salt,
pepper and nutmeg. This sauce goes very well with
fish, vegetables and meat.

CLOVES

Cloves are the dried flower buds of the clove tree which is native to Indonesia (the Moluccas), Madagascar, and Zanzibar in east Africa.

The buds of the clove are harvested before they flower, and then dried. The round central part contains an essential oil, essence of clove. If the clove is of good quality, the oil flows from it when it is plunged into water. You can also test a clove's freshness by pressing it between your fingers. If the oil bubbles out when you squeeze, the clove is fresh.

Cloves are very aromatic. You can buy them whole or powdered. They are included in a number of aromatic mixtures, such as spicy bread and cold spiced meat. They can also be added to braised beef and vegetables such as red cabbage and beetroot. In Holland, the Dutch produce a cheese flavoured with cloves. Cloves can also be used to flavour fruit dishes, especially apple pie, as well as cakes and gateaux, liqueurs, mulled wine, cinnamon wine and punch.

Cloves are good for the digestion. Biting on a clove also relieves toothache.

RED WINE MARINADE

27 fl oz (750 ml) water · 1 tbsp
(1 x 15 ml spoon) salt · 10 peppercorns ·
3 cloves · 4 juniper berries · 1 bay leaf ·
carrots · leeks · celery · 2 onions ·
12 fl oz (350 ml) red wine · 5 fl oz
(150 ml) red wine vinegar

Add the herbs and spices to the water and bring to the boil. Clean and cut up the vegetables, then wash and drain them. Peel and chop the onions. Put the vegetables and onions into the water and boil for 10 minutes. Add the red wine and the wine vinegar and leave to cool. This marinade is suitable for game. The meat should marinate for 3 to 4 days. Do not forget to turn the meat at regular intervals.

TEA PUNCH

16 fl oz (500 ml) water · 2 tbsps
(2 x 15 ml spoons) tea leaves · a small
stick of cinnamon · 3 cloves · 16 fl oz
(500 ml) red wine · 3 oz (75 g) sugar ·
1 glass rum · juice of 1 orange ·
juice of ½ lemon

Bring the water to the boil. Warm a teapot, put in the tea, cloves and cinnamon, and fill with boiling water. Leave to infuse for 5 minutes. Heat the wine, rum, lemon and orange juice. Do not allow the mixture to boil. Strain the tea, add the wine and leave the punch to infuse in a covered pan.

PEPPER

The three types of pepper that we use, black pepper, white pepper and green pepper, are all found on the same plant. They come from a climbing plant which produces berries.

 To make black peppercorns, the berries are dried before they are mature. Black pepper has a very distinctive flavour. White peppercorns are made from the ripe berries which are dried after the red skin surrounding them has been removed. Although it is not as strong, white pepper is very aromatic. Black and white peppers are sold as peppercorns or as ground pepper.

Green peppercorns are the immature berries preserved in brine. The flavour of fresh green pepper is less sharp but is still very distinctive. The brine gives it a salty taste.

Pink peppercorns are also preserved in brine. Pink pepper is made in the same way as white pepper but the red skin is left on the berry. It has a very delicate flavour. You can also buy pink pepper and green pepper in dried form. Green pepper is dried slowly so that the skin does not go black. Green and pink pepper are often mixed with white or black pepper.

When it is ground, pepper very quickly loses its flavour and aroma. Ground pepper should always be kept in a sealed container so that air cannot get to it. All of these types of peppers can be used to add piquancy to cooking. Pepper has the best flavour when it is freshly ground in a pepper mill.

Peppercorns can also be used whole. They are removed at at the end of the cooking time.

PEPPER SAUCE

1 tbsp (1 x 15 ml spoon) butter ·
½ onion, chopped · 1 tbsp (1 x 15 ml
spoon) mustard · 4 fl oz (100 ml) dry
white wine · 8 fl oz (250 ml) meat stock
or meat juice · 1 tbsp (1 x 15 ml spoon)
Cognac · 7 fl oz (200 ml) single cream ·
salt · 1 tbsp (1 x 15 ml spoon) ground
white pepper · 2 tbsps (2 x 15 ml
spoons) green peppercorns

Heat the butter and brown the onion. Add the mustard
and wine. Bring to the boil, reduce the heat and add
the stock or meat juice, the Cognac and the cream.
The sauce should not now be allowed to boil otherwise it may curdle. Season with salt, ground pepper
and peppercorns. Simmer for 5 minutes. Delicious
with grilled, braised, sautéed, smoked or roast meats.

SWEET AND SOUR CUCUMBERS

2¼ lb (1 kg) cucumbers · 1¾ pints
(1 litre) water · salt · 7 fl oz (200 ml)
wine vinegar · 9 oz (250 g) sugar · small
piece of cinnamon · 2 cloves · 5 white
peppercorns

Peel the cucumbers and cut them in half lengthways.
Cut the halves in two lengthways and remove the
seeds. Cut into chunks 5 cm long. Bring 1¼ pints
(700 ml) salted water to the boil, add the cucumber
pieces and cook for 5 minutes. Drain in a collander.
In another saucepan, bring the vinegar, the rest of the
water, the sugar, cinnamon, cloves and peppercorns
to the boil. Boil the mixture for about 5 minutes. Fill
some clean preserving jars with the cucumber pieces.
Strain the liquid, bring to the boil and pour straight
onto the cucumber. Seal the jars.
Store in a cool place and leave for at least 15 days.
Delicious with fish and meat.

CURRY

Curry is a mixture of different spices, carefully blended. According to the recipe books, it is made up of 12 or 13 spices and herbs.

The main spices and herbs used in curry powder are chilli, aniseed, bay leaves, cumin seeds, cardamom, cinnamon, cloves, coriander, ginger, nutmeg, and turmeric.

The flavour of curry depends on the particular mix of spices. You can buy containers of curry powder but it is often best to make your own, following a recipe. Nowadays, of course, you can also buy good curries in a supermarket.
Oriental shops sell different mixtures of curry spices. Some mixtures are mild, others are very hot. The darker the colour, the stronger the flavour. Curry can be used in sauces and soups, and with meat, chicken, fish, vegetables and potato dishes.
Curry stimulates the action of the glands, the stomach and the intestines. Opposite you will find a marvellous curry mix to make at home.

MADRAS

1 tbsp (1 x 15 ml spoon) ground
coriander · 2 tsps (2 x 5 ml spoons)
garlic powder · 1 tbsp (1 x 15 ml spoon)
ground cumin · 2 tsps (2 x 5 ml spoons)
ground turmeric · 1 tsp (1 x 5 ml)
powdered ginger · ½ tsp (0.5 x 5 ml
spoon) powdered chilli · 1 tsp (1 x 5 ml
spoon) cayenne pepper · 1 tbsp
(1 x 15 ml spoon) salt · 1 tbsp (1 x 15 ml
spoon) ground black pepper · ½ tbsp
(0.5 x 15 ml spoon) mustard powder ·
small pinch ground saffron

Put all the ingredients into a jar with a screw-on lid.
Shake vigorously. This delicious curry mixture is a
good replacement for ordinary curry powder.

EGGS IN CURRY SAUCE

16 fl oz (500 ml) chicken stock ·
2 onions, chopped · 3 tbsps (3 x 15 ml
spoons) cayenne pepper · 1 clove garlic,
crushed · 3 tsps (3 x 5 ml spoons) curry
powder (Madras) · 1 small tin tomato
purée · salt · 4 hard-boiled eggs

Put all the ingredients, except the eggs, in a saucepan. Bring to the boil while stirring. Season with salt.
Shell the eggs and cut them in half lengthways. Lay
the egg halves in the sauce and heat. Serve with rice
or French bread and a green salad.

PAPRIKA

Paprika is a sweet red capsicum which is native to Central and South America. There are several different types of powdered paprika, most of which are produced in Hungary.

Sweet paprika is bright red. The powder is made from the ripe fruit after the seeds and arils have been removed. These are put back in later after the elimination of the bitter substances they contain. Extra-sweet paprika is made in the same way but its colour is not quite as bright and it tastes a little more bitter.

Pink paprika powder is made from the whole fruit including the seeds and arils. It is dark in colour and has a bitter flavour.

Extra-strong pink paprika is made in the same way as pink paprika but with more seeds and arils added. The flavour is very piquant.

Paprika powder should be kept away from direct light in a sealed container, otherwise its flavour and colour soon disappear. The quantity used depends on the pungency of the paprika.

Meat should never be coated with paprika because the powder caramelises at high temperatures and becomes bitter. It should always be cooked at a low temperature.

Paprika powder adds savour to sauces for meat and rice dishes and it is this ingredient which gives goulash its distinctive flavour. Paprika helps digestion and stimulates the action of the glands.

CHILLIS

Chilli is the fruit of another type of capsicum tree. It is related to the pepper and belongs to the Solanaceae family. You can buy green or red chillis. The seeds of red chilli are very hot.

The smaller the chilli, the stronger the flavour. The smallest chillis are preserved and sold in pots. They have a particularly strong flavour and are used to prepare Indonesian dishes.

In the Indonesian kitchen, the chilli is known as 'lombok'. It is the main ingredient for many Indonesian and East Asian dishes. Dishes that contain the seeds of the chilli are often extremely hot. In western cooking, people normally remove the seeds. It is best to do this under a running tap. Never rub your eyes after seeding chillis.
Chillis are sold fresh, dried or powdered. Powdered chilli, however, has less flavour. If a recipe requires chilli and you do not have any to hand, use a little cayenne pepper. This aromatic mixture is made from ground chilli seeds. Dried chilli adds flavour to soups, stock, sauces, preserved fruit, meat and pickles. Most chillis are imported but some species can be cultivated in temperate climates.

SAFFRON

Saffron is a spice made from the dried stigmas of the saffron crocus, Crocus sativa. The saffron crocus is cultivated in Spain, the south of France and Italy.

Saffron is literally worth its weight in gold. Between 60,0000 and 80,000 flowers are needed to produce 2¼ lb (1 kg) stigmas. You can buy the dried saffron stigmas in strands or as powder.

Saffron is a bright yellow colour. Make sure that you always buy real saffron. It soon loses its flavour in a damp atmosphere, so it should be kept in a sealed container. Its adds a pleasant flavour to rice dishes, cakes, soups, particularly bouillabaisse, and many Spanish and Italian fish dishes.
Saffron also has medicinal uses. A little saffron dissolved in a glass of lukewarm water is an effective gargle for mouth and throat infections.

VANILLA

Vanilla flavouring is the dried fruit of vanilla, an orchid which is native to Mexico. Vanilla has to be cultivated in a hot climate and is grown extensively on islands in the Indian Ocean. It is mainly used in the manufacture of confectionery, ice cream and pastries.

The fruit, or pods, are harvested before they mature. The damp pods are heated and then dried. They turn into black shiny sticks and produce an oil called vanillin, which gives vanilla its delicate flavour and scent. If you split a vanilla pod, you will see the black, aromatic core.

A stick of vanilla is expensive but it can be used several times. After use, simply rinse it in cold water and keep it in a sealed container. It can also be stored in sugar. The sugar becomes impregnated with the aroma of vanilla.

You can also buy synthetic vanilla in the form of vanilla sugar. Its flavour is less strong because it does not contain the essential oil of real vanilla. Another alternative is vanilla essence, which is made by infusing dried vanilla sticks in alcohol.

Vanilla is used in sweet dishes such as pastries, flans, drinks, puddings, confectionery and liqueurs. It is soothing for nervousness and agitation. Infuse a stick of vanilla in milk or in hot chocolate.

OILS, VINAIGRETTES AND INFUSIONS

AROMATIC HERB OIL

4 sprigs fresh thyme · 2 sprigs fresh
tarragon · 2 sprigs fresh basil · 2 tsps
(2 x 5 ml spoons) black peppercorns ·
4 juniper berries · 1¾ pints (1 litre)
corn oil

Rinse the herbs in cold water, drain and dry with kitchen paper. Clean 2 pint (500 ml) bottles. Scald them and leave upside-down to drain. Put 2 sprigs thyme, 1 sprig tarragon, 1 sprig basil, 1 teaspoon (1 x 5 ml spoon) peppercorns and 2 juniper berries into each bottle. Fill with oil and leave in a cool place for at least a month.

This herb oil will keep for about a year. You can use olive oil instead of corn oil, but corn oil gives the final product a more neutral flavour. This aromatic oil is delicious on a salad, in a marinade or on meat to be grilled or cooked on a barbecue.

You can also concoct other imaginative combinations of herbs and spices. You can increase the quantities given here. If you want your herb oil to have more bite, add a chilli, split lengthways, to the herbs.

AROMATIC MIXTURE

1 tbsp (1 x 15 ml spoon) powdered garlic ·
1 tsp (1 x 5 ml spoon) dried basil ·
1 tsp (1 x 5 ml spoon) dried savory ·
1 tsp (1 x 5 ml spoon) powdered onion ·
1½ tsp (1.5 x 5 ml spoon) ground
black pepper · 1 tsp (1 x 5 ml spoon)
dried sage

Put all the ingredients into a jar with a screw-on lid and shake vigorously. This is suitable for all sorts of dishes.

AROMATIC VINEGAR

1 sprig fresh thyme · 4 sprigs fresh
tarragon · 2 sprigs fresh basil · 1 red
chilli · 1 clove garlic · 2 tsps (2 x 5 ml
spoons) black peppercorns · 4 juniper
berries · 1 bottle natural white vinegar

Rinse the herbs in cold water, drain and dry with
kitchen paper. Wash the red chilli, split it lengthways
and remove the seeds. Peel the garlic clove and cut in
half. Pour the vinegar into 2 very clean pint (500 ml)
bottles. Divide the herbs and spices between the
bottles. Seal the bottles and leave the vinegar to stand
for 2 weeks. Filter before using.

ORANGE TEA PUNCH

2 oranges · 1 lemon · 16 fl oz (500 ml)
red wine · 4 cloves · 1 piece cinnamon ·
6 oz (150 g) sugar · 1 tsp (1 x 5 ml
spoon) tea leaves · 16 fl oz (500 ml)
water · 6 tbsps (6 x 15 ml spoons) rum

Squeeze the oranges and cut the lemon into slices.
Heat the orange juice, wine, cloves, sugar and cinnamon in a saucepan. Boil for about 15 minutes on a
low heat. Boil the water and infuse the tea leaves.
Pour the boiling tea into a glass carafe. Filter the wine
mixture into the tea. Add the rum, stirring all the time.
Pour the punch into glasses.

BOUQUET GARNI

Fresh herbs can be arranged in a bouquet and used in a room as an air-freshener. Herbs such as rosemary, chervil, tarragon, lemon balm, celery and chrysanthemums are ideal. A bouquet of these will not only fill a room with its fragrance but will look attractive too.

Sachets of **bouquet garni** are mainly used to flavour soup or stock without the herbs spilling into the liquid. A homemade bouquet garni is very easy to make. You simply tie together several sprigs of fresh herbs, put them into the pot and remove them at the end of the cooking time. The bouquet garni has another great advantage; not only does it add flavour and aroma to your dishes, but it allows you to experiment with different combinations of herbs.

Here are some suggestions:

4 sprigs parsley · 2 sprigs fennel ·
2 sprigs tarragon · 1 spring onion ·
a piece of leek

Tie these together and use the bouquet to flavour braised fish, soup and roast chicken.

ITALIAN BOUQUET GARNI

3 sprigs basil · 3 sprigs parsley · 1 small
onion · 1 sprig oregano

Tie together and use with Italian recipes such as minestrone, fish, roast chicken and tomato dishes.

Fresh herbs are being used more and more in the kitchen. They allow you to add unique flavours to your dishes. The more you use herbs, the more innovative you will become. This certainly goes for making bouquet garnis.

Bouquet garnis can be frozen. The herbs which freeze best are parsley, dill, basil, tarragon, savory, marjoram, thyme and rosemary. Rinse the herbs in cold water, drain and dry with kitchen paper. Arrange them in bunches and tie together. Freeze them in plastic bags. Label the bags with the names of the herbs and the date of freezing. If a recipe requires chopped herbs, you can easily split up the contents of a bag. Freezing allows you to pick herbs when they are at their best and use them at any time. You are also able to make up and freeze bouquets which best suit your ideas and your needs.

You can also **dry** herbs. Rinse them first and dab dry with kitchen paper. Hang the bunches up in a well ventilated place. When they have dried, the herbs can be crumbled and sealed in air-tight containers.

A **pot-pourri** is a mixture of dried petals, flowers, roses and spices. You can also make a pot-pourri from herbs and spices. Whether arranged in a dish or tied in a bunch, they give out a wonderful scent.
You could make an attractive pot-pourri from thyme, rosemary, bay, camomile and dried rose petals.

You can also make **sachets of herbs** to put among your clothes. Make small bags of cotton or linen, fill with them with a mixture of thyme, rosemary, mint and lemon balm. Add some dried flower petals and tie the sachets with ribbon. This makes an original present.
Fill sachets with your favourite scented herbs for the bathroom, such as lemon balm or camomile. They add a delicate scent to bath water.

SAUCES

VINAIGRETTE

Chop finely a mixture of chives, tarragon, chervil, parsley, and capers. Mix 2 tablespoons (2 x 15 ml spoons) of this mixture with 4 fl oz (100 ml) of corn oil and 2 tablespoons (2 x 15 ml spoons) of aromatic herb vinegar (page 55), salt and pepper. Beat well. This vinaigrette goes with all salads.

BASIL SEASONING

½ tsp (0.5 x 5 ml spoon) mustard ·
1½ tbsps (1.5 x 15 ml spoons) vinegar ·
3 tbsps (3 x 15 ml spoons) sunflower oil ·
salt · pepper · ½ tbsp (0.5 x 15 ml spoon)
basil sauce (pesto) · 4 basil leaves,
finely chopped

Mix all the ingredients thoroughly. Use this seasoning to flavour cheese salads, tomato salads or pasta.

CHIVE SAUCE

6 oz (150 g) white bread with the crusts
removed · 4½ fl oz (125 ml) milk ·
4 hard-boiled eggs · 4 tbsps (4 x 15 ml
spoons) chives, finely chopped · 1 tsp
(1 x 5 ml spoon) Worcestershire sauce ·
4 fl oz (100 ml) olive oil · 3 tsps (3 x 5 ml
spoons) lemon juice · 3 tsps (3 x 5 ml
spoons) mustard

Put the bread into a bowl and soak it in milk. Shell the eggs, chop finely and push through a sieve with the soaked bread (you can also use a mixer for this). Slowly add the olive oil and season with lemon juice, Worcestershire sauce and mustard. Add the chives just before serving.

DILL SAUCE

1 bunch dill, chopped · 1 oz (25 g)
butter · 1 oz (25 g) flour · 16 fl oz
(500 ml) meat stock · salt · 1 egg yolk ·
3 tbsps (3 x 15 ml spoons) single cream

Melt the butter in a frying pan, add half the chopped
dill and brown over a low heat. Add the flour and
brown for a few minutes. Add the stock, stirring constantly until the sauce is smooth and creamy, Add salt
to taste and simmer the sauce for a few minutes. Mix
the egg yolk with the cream and stir into the sauce.
Add the rest of the dill. This sauce is good with
poached fish.

PARSLEY SAUCE

4 oz (100 g) butter · 1 oz (25 g) flour ·
16 fl oz (500 ml) chicken stock · 1 bunch
parsley · a little lemon juice · 2 tbsps
(2 x 15 ml spoons) dry white wine ·
salt · pepper

Melt 1 oz (25 g) of the butter in a saucepan. Add the
flour and cook for a few minutes. Add the stock and
wine, stirring all the time. Boil for a few minutes. Add
the butter, a knob at a time. Chop the parsley finely.
When the sauce has absorbed all the butter, add the
salt, pepper, lemon juice and chopped parsley. Serve
immediately.

INDEX OF RECIPES